The

Ice

Horses

Other Poetry from Scottish Cultural Press

Scottish Contemporary Poets Series

Gerry Cambridge, *The Shell House;* 1 898218 34 X
Jenni Daiches, *Mediterranean;* 1 898218 35 8
Valerie Gillies, *The Ringing Rock;* 1 898218 36 6
Kenneth C Steven, *The Missing Days;* 1 898218 37 4
Brian Johnstone, *The Lizard Silence;* 1 898218 54 4
Siùsaidh NicNèill, *All My Braided Colours;* 1 898218 55 2
Ken Morrice, *Talking of Michelangelo;* 1 898218 56 0
Tom Bryan, *North East Passage;* 1 898218 57 9
Maureen Sangster, *Out of the Urn;* 1 898218 65 X
Anne MacLeod, *Standing by Thistles;* 1 898218 66 8
Walter Perrie, *From Milady's Wood;* 1 898218 67 6
William Hershaw, *The Cowdenbeath Man;* 1 898218 68 4

John Buchan's Collected Poems,
Andrew Lownie and William Milne (eds); 1 898218 47 1

From a Gael with no Heartland, Alan McLeod; 1 898218 62 5

News of the World: Last Poems, Maurice Lindsay; 1 898218 32 3

Canty and Couthie: Familiar and forgotten Scots poems,
collected by Anne Forsyth; 1 898218 04 8

Robert Burns: a man for all seasons, compiled by John Young;
1 898218 60 9

The

Ice

Horses

The Second Shore Poets Anthology

edited by
Stewart Conn and Ian McDonough

SCOTTISH CULTURAL PRESS

First published 1996 by
Scottish Cultural Press
Unit 14, Leith Walk Business Centre,
130 Leith Walk, Edinburgh EH6 5DT
Tel: 0131 555 5950 ◆ Fax: 0131 555 5018

British Library Cataloguing in Publication Data
A catalogue entry for this book is available from the British Library

ISBN: 1 898218 85 4

Printed and bound by
BPC-AUP Aberdeen Ltd, Aberdeen

CONTENTS

INTRODUCTION

A current received wisdom runs that, for live poetry to be entertaining and able to attract an audience, it has to be able to shout, to create a theatrical ambience, to reflect current street fashion, to somehow take its trousers down. There is a place for all of this and an important one, but there is also a place for poetry which excites the imagination in other, often quieter ways. Shore Poets was set up in 1991 to attempt to help provide a platform for spoken verse which entertained and at the same time gave pause for thought, which could take some aspects of everyday life and amplify them into something resonant and evocative. Five years on, we feel that this aim has been reached – Shore Poets monthly readings at the Fruitmarket Gallery, Edinburgh, featuring established and new voices together with a variety of music, have become a prominent feature of the Scottish literary scene, attracting a large regular audience.

The contributors to this, the second Shore Poets anthology, have been selected from among poets who have performed since the publication of the first volume,[1] and who were not featured in it. Choosing the poems was invigorating. We shared a growing excitement at the energy and variety of the material, and at what we perceived as a common thread of emotional veracity which was refreshing and heartening. Two of the poems which appear here – *The Ghost in the Snow* by Iain Crichton Smith, and *Beldorney Castle* by Valerie Gillies – were specially created for 'Poetry and Rebellion – A commemoration of the 2nd Jacobite Uprising', a special Shore Poets event held in June 1995.

We hope you enjoy the volume and will be able to join us at one of the monthly readings.

Stewart Conn/Ian McDonough
Edinburgh, August 1996

---

[1] *The Golden Goose Hour*, edited by R Brackenbury & B Johnstone (Taranis 1994).

The Ice Horses

I lean over and point my father's gaze
to the photo of Bud Finch
at the wheel of his 'Minneapolis Moline' tractor
which, though sank during the war,
has been salvaged.

Later, as a storm battered
the tin roof of our garage
and flakes of broken fence spread across our lawn,
I returned to Bud's memoirs.

One winter the Thames here froze over
and horses walked out across the river
to graze upon the reeds.
One fell through
and men from Bud's village pulled it out,
laid it on a gate, carried it back to the village.

This flashes through my mind as I cross
the same water in the passenger seat of my dad's truck.
We are working at a mental institution,
(once a military hospital)
slipping under the wooden floorboards of wards
to fireproof heating ducts with glass fibre.

We hear heavy horses above, wandering.

Later still I discover that my maternal grandfather
lay in that hospital as I was born in the winter of '59.
My mother tells me I was taken in and shown to him
like a new tractor brought onto his farm.
Did his eyes see swaddling bands, metal bed, window bars
and bare floorboards glazed with water
or did they see barn, field, horses,
folding under snow, ships sinking in a blizzard.

The severed tongue

Where's they goin' grampy?

Fondling the tin marker in the calf's ear
I felt its coat of dried mud shudder
as his hand came down once more.
The thwack sent it skidding up the planks
like a potted billiard ball.

Twenty years later
I can't grasp that tongue.
Can't get a hold of the skull
between two firm hands and prise it open.

My accent was drained out of me.
A slit bullock over a drain
taught to sound better
my nose forced down in a trough of grammar.

Those words that dripped off his tongue.
The lolling, spittly threads
of long berkshire a's and r's
were sluiced clean away.

Now I stand at a window
in Oxford's covered market
looking down through my reflection
at a tray of severed tongues.
Trying to find a bucket for his vowels.

The hare-lip

The hare-lip of my step-grandfather
cut like a chalk-stream down his face
twisting the upper lip into a V
and pulling the sides of his mouth
closer together.

To this day I'm not sure how it's spelt
h.a.r.e. or h.a.i.r.
but I do remember his dog
bolting a hare across the stubble fields
and his worn pipe trembling in that V
as he struck another match

whilst I'd sit in his front room
picking at lamb-roll school lunchtimes
listening to country voices rattling from a radio
as big as the T.V. we'd rented since 1966.

Now I get confused.
All I hear is the swish and crackle of lit straw
as I spin the dial and press my ear to the speaker.
Those days I was closer
as I peered into the warm dust
at the tiny red lights that flickered.
Could tell a false accent from a real one.
Now it's all scrambled.
Lost on the air somewhere
from those smoky valves.

Like a spitfire over the channel.

Diaspora

I.   Kurds in Bonn
      have molten eyes,
      huddle in Kino fronts,
      study broken pavements for clues.
      At night, in crowded flats,
      they dream of snow leopards.

II.   Shasta Indians
      get drunk on the steps
      of the San Francisco Public Library.
      Their cheap sugary wine
      bleeds from broken bottles,
      drop-by-drop,
      down sewers
      where no salmon run.

III.   In Wimbledon sunshine
      a giant Kerryman shakes a fist
      at the Bank of England,
      lurches between prim mothers
      in Laura Ashley frocks.
      His anger scatters the people around me —
      an Irish Moses parting a Saxon sea.

IV.   Two Lewismen
      choke on a dusty highway,
      night is falling
      on the way to Medicine Hat.
      "Chan' eil ceilidh air a' phreiridh ..."
      (there is no ceilidh on the prairie)
      Their own fathers slept in hobo boxcars
      on the Canadian Pacific,
      crammed with Blackfeet, Assiniboine and Cree.
      All seeking westwards
      a harvest none ever found.

George Stephen

(Born 1829, in Banffshire, grew up in Dufftown. Became a banker and was founder of the Canadian Pacific Railway, which joined Canada together and had a profound impact on that nation's future.)

The Canadian Pacific began in Dufftown,
Its founder, George Stephen, was nurtured there.
Aberdeen to London, he'd been around.
With his cousin, became Canada's railroad pair.
Railway. THWACK. Slavs hammering cold steel.
Railway. THWACK. Scandinavians break hard rock.
German straw bosses with wounds to heal.
Irish poker players, Chinese with opium to hock.

Bare-knuckle boxing, horseshoes, tug-of-war.
THWACK. Backs breaking, laying steel on grass.
Stephen faced bankruptcy; they'd loan no more.
But workers drove the final spike in Eagle Pass.

From Dufftown to the Pacific on a dragon of steam.
The Canadian Pacific: a Dufftown dream.

The Dark Gift

Pure white and buff flight feather, tawny owl's.
I found it by the lane as I walked home,
kept it for your interested son, its comb
and furriness, despite his adolescent scowls
and rancour, fascinating. I used to search
far woods round here, confused teenager, for
lush primaries of those birds I rarely saw,
on mornings when my mother thought the church

contained me. Tonight you drive me back
up the Glasgow road towards the city's
knives and angers, all the human pities
and our own. Dazzling road signs mark the black.
And you hit the wheel, as I clutch this tawny's feather,
as we speed on through the autumn night together.

The Drunken Lyricist

We met that grey dull evening on the east shore.
Roaring round the bend he came, flat out
at fifteen miles an hour, and slowed. We had to shout
till he turned off his engine. **It's going to pour
it looks like!**: me. **Oa, I'm haardly cancerned
thee night wi weather, man!** he said, flat cap askew.
Gap-toothed smile. Torched cheeks. Eyes, Atlantic blue.
Hiv you seen any? Weemun? Whisky burned
its golden track in him, and he would search.
's that wun, man? – the shore's dark speck.
Not waiting a reply, through the bright wreck
of that grey evening, he roared off, with a lurch.
His tractor almost reared on its back tyres.
Fifteen miles an hour flat out, parched by amber fires.

Orkney

Fire in Winter

The owner cut the row of saplings back
that January, and one afternoon piled tall
once-flourishing boughs, and torched them all
as a chill dusk moved in. Each burst and crack
later drew me out to the fire's life, from words
to gaze at summer's shade grown winter's heat,
the happy brawl of boughs being reduced to neat
manageable ash, as the winter's birds,
fieldfare and redwing, with their cries
flew high above in darkness, through the sky's
enormous anonymity. That blaze roared dry-red
my face and wintered mind until to the dark's
swabbing effortless cool I turned instead,
and Springside children's shouts, far exclamation marks.

Ayrshire

Patchwork Kingdom

Unseen my neighbours sleep.
Scissors and glue at hand
I rifle through piles of newsprint
for something or other I'd read
and thought maybe I'd keep
God knows where I saw it.
I'm struck instead by a headline
ship of dreams docks in Fife
Fife. Where I was a child
of gardens, playgrounds, beaches
and two bridges, one going north
the other south, that led
to all the places I reached
before here, a tenement block
on the other side of the firth
which my daughter knows as home.
On the other side of the window
moths, wisps of stuff
electrified by the light.
Hue of terracotta
a vase brims with buds
daylight will coax open.
A card leans against it
that my father sent my daughter
from Stornoway, on Lewis.
I'm working here this week
and I took a walk to the harbour
he writes, *and I saw fishermen*
mending their nets on the pier.
Poems, and dreams too, are stitched
on whatever thread's at hand
makeshift amalgams of
what's present, remembered, desired.

I'll hope to see you soon
concludes my dad, concludes
the poem, ship of dreams
in whose churning wake, beyond
the sleeping tenement
beyond the one-way system
and the covered shopping centre
are gleaming, wave-reflected
like stars, the lights of Fife.

Higher

"Higher!" she shouts in the links
swing-park. I push into sound
erupting like a flood-tide
as trees explode crows and
arrowed from birches, a jet
repeats itself and repeats
itself and repeats itself
through clouds above the firth
and repeats itself again and
again until we distinguish
three circling warplanes
on some kind of training run.
Unbearable at first
it soon gets so you
stop even noticing the noise.
"Higher!" she shouts. I push.

Outsider

to Jeremy Cronin

Reading the poems you gave me, I marvel
at a resolution beyond my comprehension,
the lyrical intensity
governing what you have to say.

And face pressed helplessly
against my hotel-room window,
am unable to eradicate
from my mind the glass plate

through which for one quarter
of an hour, on the day
your wife died, you saw her mother
sobbing, and could not comfort her.

                         To what
can one cling, when monstrosity
exists beyond reason?

                    Pigeons beat
their wings and walk heel-toe
on the roof below.

         The Lutheran Church opposite
is tiered like a wedding-cake,
against a dark sky.

      Whose knife is at whose throat ?

Jedibe Camp

Trust

Spiky umbels of papyrus bob against my face
as Trust, the head poler, steers through
channels scarcely wide enough to take us.
Reaching an island of baobab, Trust places

a finger to his lips, points at a silhouette
bunched high on a fork: a Pels fishing owl.
I can just pick it out – a blotch of cinnamon
and white. Trust gives the thumbs-up.

Poling the mokoro back across the lagoon
he says he hopes his son will go to school
(which he didn't) and learn to read and write
(as his father did, in the diamond mine).

He names the water-birds in his own tongue
and Latin; showing no bitterness
at working, after deductions for food
and board, for a miserly daily rate.

Next day on the plane, I'll find myself seated
behind a lady who "came all the way from Minnesota
just to see the Pels: worth every cent, believe me":
member of neither a rare nor an endangered species.

Water Two

Our boat moored to the reeds, Water Two
catches three tiger-fish, myself none.
Nor the elderly Zimbabwean in the bow.
Suddenly at 7 a.m., we are into a shoal

of barbel. After three revolutions
my reel screams, then slackens –
the leader bitten through. I land a bream.
The mozzies take over. "Tiger next time!"

Alongside our catch, on the grass,
instead of the customary fly-box
the size 6 shoe of a former Miss South Africa
here on a promotional tour. In the small hours

I think of her stretching those lissom limbs;
while in the next tent the Zimbabwean
laments Mugabe's latest sequestrations.
Hourly, the snuffle of hippo

in the surrounding swamp. Already, Okavango
a jewel, in the brain. After coffee and fruit,
I find my backpack speckled with birdshit.
The previous day's catch, fish-eagle bait.

Over the Desert

Entering the Kalahari the pure waters
of the Delta, rather than form an estuary,
peter out in a depth of sand so great
even major earth tremors leave no trace

but are absorbed before reaching the surface.
Subjecting our lives, scarcely
more substantial, to varied analogy:
refreshment, or drought, of the spirit;

placing ourselves at others'
disposal; from this, to loss
of enlightenment over the centuries.
Below, a terrain *in extremis*,

dry valleys and fossil dunes
extending to the horizon and beyond;
the world's curve, billions of sandgrains.
Through a blur of condensation

imagine mirage-like, hazy and wavery,
an ancient Bushman and his wife, alone
in the thornveld, awaiting the hyenas
through whom they will join their ancestors.

Lochgilphead lights

You bring in wood
and cold clings to your arms.
'The stars have come out,' you say,
as if stars are in or out at will,
as if volition lights the sky.

Across the loch
house and street are a chorus
of light, each note
the water duplicates,
while the frosted ground repeats
the singing sky.
At the impact of a log
the fire showers light
borrowed from the sun.

It is the last night
of the year, and the light here,
in this small arc of ours,
seems of our own will,
unbound by earth and water,
beyond the strength of stars.

Sunday morning, Mission San Jose

Song leaps from the creamy stone,
carried by wind which dishevels the breath
of doves. A train whistle floats
in the sunlight, and bells above all, raising
the voices, the vivacious guitars and softly
tapping high-heels. Under a tree,
where the leaves tremble and the vanished past
mingles with every thread of sound.
Women in Sunday clothes move
mildly through cloisters and the curve of arches.

I am almost deceived. For it's green where Indians
laboured and learned the conquerors' songs,
and the sun is a rich balm, and there's peace
in this beautiful place. Our broken century
has brought tranquillity. The cowboy has hung up
his spurs and holds his woman's hand.
The girls have ribbons in their hair. The priest
smiles, even on me, idolator,
consoled, yet thinking of the misbegotten
care that masks reality.

Windfalls

The mower nudging under the apple trees
splits tiny windfalls. The sour reek

of apples mingles with sweet grass and colours
of angled sunlight, gift of this northern quarter.

The air is generous. The blades flick daisy
and buttercup sequins and stir the smell of pine

into the rhythm of summer, of evening, of mowing.
Doves croon in the woods. Perhaps I'm too easily

pleased or out of kilter in a world gnawed
by greed. Perhaps I too readily temper the task

to a small garden and offer the stealthy shock
of pleasure to millions who know or think they suffer.

CHRISTINE DE LUCA

In the mind's eye

Jutland, 1995

I can close my eyes now and see
bikes spin past stiff wheat,
past barley combed by a warm wind.
In the haze, wide-angled, can gaze
at cows in salt shallows, standing
dark against light-bleached land
as they have stood for centuries,
Cuyp or Vermeer-like.

And by a lake at Hampen,
the deep focus in the mind's eye
of wind on silk reeds
and the swither of dragon flies,
a surprise of blueness.

This landscape is primeval,
ancient, fluvio-glacial:
a shard of time defining space.

All evening the irrigation wheel pulses,
moves imperceptibly. Jets of water
parabola towards a moon, I remember,
sickled gold on lavender.

Hallowe'en hansel

A boannie nicht for castin kale:
a fat mön vaegin owre Sannis,
a hale gadderie o laads an lasses.

A spree i der blöd,
laads loupit dykes
purled kale-stocks
iggit een anidder on
ripe da rigs
hunse fur hens
whit a stramash
an dan da dash
tae a porch door
lift da sneck
ball in da booty
rin like da mellishon
dunna look back.

But dee an me
pooskered wi da bassel
fell ahint ta draa breath,
taste wir first smoorikin.
But aa I can mind is da mön
gaffin at me in mi cöttikins
wis ahint an uncan barn
an dy blett hansel
anunder a kendlin o starns.

Glossary:

vaegin: *voyaging*; spree: *jollification*; purled: *poked, lifted with fingers*;
hunse: *rummage*; stramash: *commotion*; da mellishon: *the devil*;
pooskered: *exhausted*; bassel: *struggle*; smoorikin: *kiss*; gaffin: *laughing*;
cöttikins: *ankle socks*; uncan: *unfamiliar*, dy: *your* (familiar form)

CHRISTINE DE LUCA

Farmad

Ged nach toirinn esan a-mach as an dìg
tha farmad agam rithe
oir chì mi na sùilean
nach eil beàrnan na cridhe-se
air sgàth 's gu bheil e còmhla rithe.

Chan e esan a tha mi 'g iarraidh
ach an deàlradh a tha na sùilean.

Envy

Although I wouldn't take him out of the ditch
I'm envious of her
because I can see in her eyes
that she has no gaps in her heart
while he is with her.

It isn't him I want
but the sparkle that's in her eyes.

Gathan

An e sin e ?
Aon bhlas de mhìlseachd
a dh' fhàg mo bheatha
nas searbha
nuair a bha e seachad.

An robh mi nas fheàrr dheth
le bruadar den bhlas
agus ciamar a bhitheadh e,
na eòlas a bhi agam
air mil chaochlaideach a' ghaol
's na gathan a dh' fhàgas e 'na dhèidh ?

Stings

Is that it?
One taste of sweetness
that left my life
more bitter
when it was over.
Was it better
to just dream of the sweetness
and how it would be,
than to taste the fickle honey of love
and the sting it leaves behind ?

Sìol an Dòchais

Sìol chruaidh
sìthean a' chait fhiadhaich
a' tuiteam air na lòin.

Boinneagan troma
uisge a' bualadh
air an rathad.

Gaoth fhuar
a' bìdeadh 's a' dol seachad
a' durraghan.

An oidhche air tuiteam
ach mo chridhe ag éirigh.

Tha'n dorchadas timchioll orm
ach chan eil e unnam:
tha 'ghrian air tilleadh
gu m' inntinn.

Seeds of Hope

Hard dandelion seeds
falling
into the puddles.

Heavy drops
of rain
hitting the road.

A cold wind
biting and passing,
growling.

Night has fallen
but my heart rises.

Darkness around me
but not inside me:
sunshine has returned
to my mind.

ANNE C FRATER

21

Fàsach

Aon shithean brèagha
a' fosgladh anns an fhàsach.

Sin an gaol a bh' agam ort-sa.

Ach cha do mhair am blàth
ach aon latha àlainn,
's nuair a shearg e
bha am fàsach
nas fhalamh buileach.

Desert

One lovely flower
opening in the desert.

That was the love I had for you.

But the blossom only lasted
for one beautiful day,
and when it withered
the desert
was emptier than ever.

Beldorney Castle

NOTE: I made this poem for the Shore Poets' Jacobite Evening. I enjoy translating the poetry of Sileas na Ceapaich very much: she is one of the finest Gaelic poets, direct and graceful. I visited her former home, Beldorney Castle, to record a programme of her poetry for BBC Radio Scotland.

Sileas was born about 1660, the aristocratic daughter of the 15th chief of the Macdonalds of Keppoch. Her father and brothers were poets in the Gaelic world. She left Lochaber to marry Gordon of Beldorney. After the failure of the Jacobite risings, Sileas' grandson James settled in Spain, where he began a sherry exporting business, and her descendants are there to this day.

Beldorney Castle

When the sun warms the field
the moss issues a mist,
the Deveron's shallows yield
a stone that fills the fist.

A long drive over the Cabrach
almost into Strathbogie
in a hired car to her castle,
the fir flower of Beldorney.

What'll we say, Sileas,
if we meet at your old home,
"Let's ride abreast
and hear each other's poems?"

Our hostess, more than kind,
says, "I know what it's like:
you talk about Sileas
as if you saw her last night."

Though she's not here,
on painted walls we trace
a horseman's leg-greave,
a lutenist's hand and face,

a kilted matchstick man
with cap and claymore,
a highlander on the hill,
wildwood, baskethilted sword.

Here a woman spoke in tune
who could praise or keen.
In her room today
her song plays with the stream.

We can see through the trees
close by the waterside
the walled yard she watched
after her child died.

Standing at her window
recalls her three-year trance
to inspire her poetry
when she neither ate nor drank.

Daughter of the fifteenth chief,
she composed full strength
battle poems, night hymns,
reports of birth and death.

In her panelled room,
although she isn't here,
when Crisdean sings in Gaelic
the oaken walls have ears.

In her restored house
while waiting to record,
I'm saying her poem over
when she revives the words.

An echo in the house
wants to keep us, cannot,
a light still in the air
ardent as our patriot.

She made heroic songs
but the Jacobites lost all,
those Gordons are in Spain now,
as Condé de Mirasol,

in a castle like Beldorney
he is remembering his loss,
when the sun warms the field,
mist issues from the moss.

The Rink

Light plays on the Rink,
on birches in the broch, its outer wall.
You are here with me in silence.

A doe hare comes this way, in no hurry,
not expecting to find humans here,
loping close enough to touch.

Her warm brown back blends
with the feather-grass, her fur
a burr-elm of reds and yellows.

After her come two jack hares,
one solid, one spindly, following her trail
with twists and turns, tides to her moon.

Most marvellous, moving smoothly,
the run of the hares is the lie of the land.
There are times when the creature is a ghost.

We think they have all gone,
till we turn and look behind us:
in the shadow of a shadow

a golden hare rests in the birchwood,
touched thousands and thousands
of times by the sun.

Over Vitebsk
After Chagall

Grandfather came home early from a war
that had never been. I remember he looked
quite regimental in his winter coat

and battered postman's cap, as he dangled
like gathered smoke between the rooftops
and the sky. I was roused by the rap

of his white stick on our slates. Behind me
a voice hissed: *"He's calling
our names, I think. Listen!"*

And I think he was: softly at first, but quite
insistently. The moon of his face bleached
green by the chlorine gas and cold.

Then suddenly nothing seemed straight
any more. Dawn spiralled in flames.
Snow curved through the runnel of our street.

The Market Square (no longer square)
had gently liquefied into a milky lens.
Even the steeple where he moored himself

was yawing crazily above its arc of little graves.
He called out again with greater urgency,
and not just our names, but something like:

. . . something *'man'* and then *'land'* and then something
'gone' . . . Though we craned in the yard with our ears
cupped, we still couldn't make him out.

The youngsters lobbed rocks and insults
as he raved: *"Where's your rifle, Grandad?"*
"Show us a skull!"

Gobs of spittle began to drench us – they reeked
of a thin despair – so we wafted our caps and bonnets,
winnowed his chaff away.

"Peace at last, praise God" whispered Nana,
crossing herself again, as the last few strands
of his message darkened the earth, like rain.

Nimbus
i.m. Davy Brown

In Tibetan Buddhism, the symbol for the mind's creative power
is not a light bulb, as in the Beano, but a cloud.
And I've heard that in Mexico they believe the dead
may speak from their graves for a short while after rain.
But Skye is nothing like Mexico.
They would never fall silent here.
Then perhaps it's true.

When I was seven, my father explained
how the dead converse through the telegraph wires
and it's only because we're stuck with being alive
that we can't understand what they say.
When I hugged the pole with him and listened,
their speech was thin and distant, but as heavenly as song.

A friend once described how he stood above Bernisdale
in a winter storm and watched the waves beat themselves
white against the gale, then surge up into the sky and disappear.
He said a blackface ewe went floundering past his door like
            tumbleweed.

I believe whatever has been done can only be translated, never
            undone.
That day, rain tasted salt at Invermoriston.

She is learning her hands

She is learning her hands
like a flute player
with the little finger perched
on an inch of thin air
above the last stop.

She is playing arpeggios slowly
each finger depressing
a hammer of air
onto silence.
She has perfect pitch.

She is examining the find
of her hand's back,
levelled for the light's fall,
her rosetta stone
with the clue to creation.

She is closing her hands
on the feel of her fingers,
discovering cushions of palm,
seeing how far you can come
without skin touching.

She is tucking her thumb
between index and middle finger,
cat's tongue
left out
when she curls into sleep.

She is learning the space
between what the eyes see
and the hands grasp,
assured of an arm's length
five fingers' dimensions.

She is timing the gaps
within touch
testing one hand with another,
finding what touches is touched,
like a lover.

My Mother Mrs Malaprop

my mother
                mrs malaprop
slept oppersite
                a chester drawers
and dreamt of
                waterfolds

she took me to
                walter disney
and had friends
                with moods
because they were
                frostrated

she came from
                kensintin
and talked about
                the muse
and lived above
                the rolls

at fortnum
          mazin
and at madame
          buckmasters
she served
          dressis

and refused to try
          a swimsuit on
for edward
          prince of wales
but at wittrin
          swam in the tablecloth

marryin my father
          she came down
her mother
          said
and set the dog
          on him

but she had class
          enough
for five of us
          and on the teliphone
played oppersite
          ivornovello

or sprague
          who waited
hopelessly
          and long
throughout
          my childhood

marryin
          for a second time
at seventy
          she told me
we dont just sit holdin hands
          you know

as wayward
          in her way with truth
as in her spellin
          she just went
for a lay down
          and died

and would have lied
          to death
that she was childless
          just in case
it helped

Seagulls

We are the dawn marauders.
We prey on pizza. We kill kebabs.
We mug thrushes for breadcrusts
with a snap of our big, bent beaks.
We drum the worms from the ground
with the stamp of our wide, webbed feet.
We spread out, cover the area –
like cops searching for the body
of a murdered fish-supper.
Here we go with our hooligan yells
loud with gluttony, sharp with starvation –
we are greedy for our survival.
Here we go bungee-jumping on the wind
charging from the great grey air.
This is invasion. This is occupation.
Our flags are black, white and grey.
Our wing-stripes are our rank.
No sun can match the brazen
colour of our mad yellow eyes.
We are the seagulls.
We are the people.

Jenny Long Legs

I lie in the darkness and listen
to some threadbare life in our room,

some fretful other life in our room
(it isn't you it isn't me)

at times like a breathless trust
or the spatter of a hesitant rain;

the caresses of feverish shadows;
the asthma of a dying candle;

(it isn't me it isn't you).
Can't you hear it there it is again:

the sparse effervescence of the wind
in the branches of a leafless tree;

the whispered insinuation
of your dress against your skin.

You say: It's just
the jenny-long-legs, that's all.

I know. Though even that
sounds more description than name.

In my cupped hand it is
some scarce yearning grown restless:

some desire searching for a gesture;
a love yet to find its word.

The Likeness

I want the wind to sound
like the wind – not to keen
as it's keen on doing in
wind that sounds like Poetry.

I want the literal sea, the sky
without its adjective, a few
honest shells – not the kind
that pretend to be ears.

And all this is here for me
on the shore at Prestonpans:
that flat grey scape of sea
shuns all comparison.

But from fishcrate smithereens,
in a moment drained of time,
I am noticed by an eye of wood
rimmed by an eyelid of rime

and the likeness is good.
Who am I to suppose I am not
a detail in a poem by driftwood,
the monologue of a rope?

Worse – maybe I exist only
as a gap in the bored smalltalk
between a couple of lonely
bits of out-of-work breezeblock.

I walk the tideline between
a great notion and its effects
eyeing the undescribed sand
with a grain of respect.

BRIAN McCABE

Kite

No matter that I am fragile –
I continually risk my neck
just to stay where I'm not.

My life is brief a loop-the-loop
a figure-eight, bound to end
in a crashed catastrophe.

But I am a purpose.
Why else does my colour's quick
tug intently at your eye?

To gather the open sky
into your mind's shuttered room
unravelling my rippling arrow.

I point at nothing but the vast
openness inside you. I am
a pennant of your desire;

I say play with me, play me.
I say hold me, let me go.
Hold me –

BRIAN MCCABE

STUART A PATERSON

Self Portraits
Rampside 1993

Not a heavyweight kestrel as I'd first thought,
but a peregrine, unravelling my small knot

of concentration, flew to within eight feet,
then punched its way over Roa Island's caus'y street.

And that golden pheasant on a Lakeland fell
turned out to be common, caught in a spill

of rare summer sun – exotic illusion,
result of wish and weather's brief collision.

This small child prammed in a Barrow street might
not after all have his or her foregone birthright

stitched into torn knees and hand-me-down knickers
and tenement toilets on Whalney by *Vickers*

or graduate these small ends that they mean
eighty-thousand man-hours painting submarines.

Down by Morecambe Bay a man has just died,
artist, friend to friends, not too old, with an eye

for the paled underbelly of the peregrine,
the seed-store that's a 'castle' on Piel Island,

for himself too, as his studio illustrates –
a small brown wing in the right eye of each self-portrait.

I never knew you John Helm, though our friends
tell me you went off quietly, elsewhere, at the end.

How like you, a man to go I must imagine
going, over our heads like that peregrine,

or kestrel perhaps to unbinoculared eyes,
discovering the distance from land to sky.

37

Old Photograph

I can look at this photograph
many times, always increasing
differences between the two men.
Chris Grieve, kindly young, staring at

the camera, hooded eyes alive
to the moment. Ezra Pound, old,
older than God, a kenspeckled
everyman, rumpled, gazing down

left at something gone. Arm in arm,
it's as if they've come together
momentarily by some trick
of superimposition. The hand

on Pound's arm looks disconnected.
Though just seven years divided
births, their features are crystal and
sand, a flash-photographer's

nightmare. One face clear, tie knotted,
forehead fresh, the other scarved and
hatted, two dark-veined cheeks
and white beard blurring black and white

humanity. It could almost
be Zeus about to take coffee
with Homer in Florian's Café
in a photo-processed woodcut.

No nationality is in
evidence, Grieve looking to long
futures, Pound on the turning away
from modern to his greatest pasts.

Arm in arm, this record will fade
divisionally; Grieve's bright face,
Pound's sloughing realisation of
one hand forever appearing
to hold him up.

Kingfisher

(for Linda Fairlie)

A multicoloured spitfire headlongs straight
down to the water quicker than an eye
could follow, spears and darts back to a branch,
itself the line and reel, the swarm its fly.

A piece of broken sky that looks to fall
unfanfared, or an Australasian
bird of paradise in impossible
surroundings till it fires the river basin,

revealing edges of too tightly-drawn
a world, wings pushing out the wider screen.

Galston 1995

Fred

During our homoerotic phase those
pellucid sentences from the Latin primer
suited us, if only in retrospect,

to perfection. *The old men watch*
the young soldiers swimming. The young men
sharpen their spears in preparation

for war. We thrilled to a fin de siècle
camp quality we were years from naming.
After their simplicity, the unseen passages

of Caesar's Gallic Wars were dark
and full of dangers. *These things being so*
Caesar set out for the land of the Helvetii

where he pitched camp in the verb
and sent his men out to forage for meaning.
Fred Scott was our teacher then. Sixth years

with five o'clock shadows quaked
in a dark stairwell outside his room,
chanting to each other like starlings:

dic duc fac fer; dicite ducete
facete ferte, greenbacked grammar books
flapping in their hands. My decision

was to Decline and Fall early,
to leave the cleverer boys to sweat it out,
with each correct answer inching along

to the period's end till their inevitable
calamitous mistake and the chill chasm
of ignorance yawned for them too.

Fred was small, neat, elegantly dressed
in grey suits, striped shirts (with white
detachable collars), whose cuffs he regularly

tugged. An early breakdown, it was rumoured,
had led to his rigidity. But Fred said
he was training our minds – a Challenge

as he was forever intimating.
You've got the brain of a hen Pow.
And do you know the thing about a hen Pow?

No sir. It hasn't got one. I was not alone.
I've seen more intelligent faces in cows
mooning over a dyke: this the look of brains

engorged on irregular verbs. Allan boy,
he said one day with his small man's
big deep voice to one whose adjective

had not agreed with its noun; Allan boy
do you walk along Princes Street
on a Wednesday afternoon with one shoe on

and one shoe off? Jocky was a gangling loon,
ever amiable. His thin shoulders shook
with his own impending wit. Haw haw sir

I don't haw haw walk along Princes Street
on a Wednesday afternoon. A silence
befell the class much as you get in a game

when a leg break rings out like a pistol shot
and an echo of pain hits everyone at once.
Our shoulders hunched. Fred cocked his head

momentarily bemused as his blue eyes
grew large. Then he had Jocky by the hair
and his head twisted down so that Jocky

was peering up his proud Roman nose.
Allan boy don't try to be witty with me
because you haven't the intelligence

to be witty. Yes sir. No sir. Three
years later the new school was opened
and all we sixth years helped in the move.

Pete and I were allocated to Fred.
He gave us money for juice and told us
of his Roman holiday. At the end of the day

he was the only one to say thank you.
His soul lies with a hundred spearheads now
coffined under glass. Their points may still

look sharp, yet if the conditions aren't
just so and young men try to sharpen them,
they will surely crumble in their hands.

Jenny in July

rolls off the mat, escapes
into the shade of a thicket
of broom. Grass feels

cool on bare arms
and legs, as her hands, still
clumsy as paws, swim

through tall stems, almost
bring heavy seed-heads
to her milky lips. She'll learn.

For now, she's the most
defenceless of all summer's
creatures, abandoned

Tom Pow

on a green doorstep
by a father who'd once
dreamed of his daughter

brushed by a fistful
of herbs, rolled in pastry
light as air, cooked

in the wink of an eye.
None of it had bothered
her at all – or him – the dish

was simply a thought –
how tender! how sweet!
Now the yellow stitches

of nipplewort shine
over her, always out of reach,
as she kicks herself ever

further into the world
of flowers and of foxes
along her rich riverbed.

The Ghost in the Snow

They were all plunged into Culloden
and the exact radiance of the guns,

those ragamuffins with claymores
who surged on their unstylish course

forward towards cannon. How cold it was.
The foggy snowstorm and the ice

blinded them. And the Royal guns
scythed them like grass. Poor peons,

peasants, hungry men, you came
to where technology struck the poem,

reality holed romance. Where was He,
elegant adolescent. Where was He

who dreamed his dream of royalty –
and ended in inconstancy –

whose mistress was a gamesome war,
for whom chiefs, men, laid down their bare

bowed heads to the executioner

long after you turned easily away
towards romantic caves, boats, Skye,

en route for warm Italy.

Boy, boy, that was what you were
in love with heather, stones, guns, air,

you moved through them like a dream in powder,

a ghost really, not with the precise weight
of a Murray or a Cumberland. Hume might write

that there are no connections, but there are,
consequences too.
                    They plunged into the mire,

these good loyal trustful men.
In rags, with scythes, crofters in their ruin,

displaced persons, who ignorantly traced
your eager boyish footsteps into frost

snow, ice, lastly the shallow grave

while a dreadful bell finally rang.
This was the end of an old song.

Money didn't tempt those rawboned wrecks

into betrayal, or the loyal lairds
whose heads shrank on gibbets, and whose beards

streamed like snow.
                    How much you asked of them,
thoughtless boy. Lost, they lose home

estate and name.
                    A glacial wind howls
around Culloden. All those early wills

are blown away on the tremendous gale.
Beautiful the snowdrop from the skull,

the daisy from the skeleton.
                    History's spade
is busy in the earth. And trade

fashions its own language. Gaelic fades
mistily like bluebells. General Wade

links his forts like a necklace of hard stone.
Death or silence fails.
                          Now soldiers burn
to serve the Empire that destroyed their homes.
They surge on foreign villages with their drums

and history again obscures like smoke
their poor thatched houses.
                          All that we can say

is that the poor must lose. Always there is
hail and snow blowing in their faces,

always a Culloden where the guns
cast giant shadows, and the broken peons

run for shelter.
                          And history is turned
topsy turvy. All that we have learned

about a hero lost in misty Skye
teaches the southern tourists how to cry

and students too with Hanovarian packs

climb the blue peaks, and don't forget the axe

of a journey predestined to defeat
as far as Derby: diminishing: as fact

stood up in daylight, stark as a skull.
The dream was after all not possible

though they crossed icy rivers. Trade repels
notions of loyalty, and the bourgeois tills

ring stronger than the sword.
                          The silly Prince
hits the wall of fact, the steel fence

of Culloden flashing fire, and discipline
clicking clearly its rehearsed routine.

Drunken sot, I hope you endlessly suffer

for the sufferings your boyish game caused
for there is cause and cause and cause

as headless men cry, as the Duke burns
the Highlands into poor threadbare ruins

while you, paunchy one, drink port,
beached, becalmed, rusted. May fierce thought

of baulked ambition thorn you, as you turn
easily away from red Culloden

towards the misty islands. Adolescent,
you spun away from graves into the wind

to a meagre rocky landscape.
                              So, go,
and leave heads to rot, ignorant beau,

powdered Narcissus.
                         May you rot in port,
swollen carcass,
                         and a mimic court

whisper 'shame', adolescent ghost
who gamed briskly so that many lost

lives, lands, wives, reason, just for you –
unread, ignorant, palpably untrue.

Poor loyal men it is for them I weep
who stumbled down history's slope

towards the cannon and the axe.

IAIN CRICHTON SMITH

Oh we must learn a cold and serious gaze
at the "great man's" grandiose ideas

however handsome and however young,
though newspapers should praise him or though song,

though his face should shine down at us from Sky
like a nice doctor's: yet we must not die

for his 'spheres of influence' or 'friendly fire'
or for his God, in gallantry, expire

or for his gloire be butchered to the bone
and hung like pigs in the wind's monotone

interrogate history. Simply recall
your own unique and irreplaceable

individuality. And so don't die
for such romance, aesthetic casuistry,

but in the real though dull at times engage
and do not for the great man make a charge

electric though it be through hail and snow
where history blows back at you, and blows

the hero from the field to wave farewell
to those who rose and then uniquely fell.

Shedding skins

Eyes whitewashed
you're blind to what's before you,
your mind on a change of image
as you separate the past from your future.

When I reach out my hand
the movement has you in a sightless panic
and frantic tongue flickering
you slide back to the safety of a dark crevice.

I get the message –
PRIVATE
NO ENTRY
You're closed for redecoration.

But later unseen
I watch
as you prepare glistening scales
for the unveiling ceremony.
You yawn abruptly   stretch   and rub
not eyes but mouth
against a stone.
An impossible smile splits your face,
widens to peel back from your head

and you emerge to leave
a skin which retains only an appearance of you.

You can discard your past,
disown it.

But I must take the husk
and put it in a box with all the others,
to be brought out someday
to crumble in my hands.

(For a few days before shedding its skin, a snake's eyes cloud over, virtually
blinding it.)

999

The apple is in my hand
as the siren's distant sound
closes in,
responding to another
preventable tragedy.

I hold the fruit
under running water,
(which only seems pure),
and wash from its green skin
the poisons we use to kill
the poisons we perceive.

And as I bite,
chalk outlines appear in the dust

ACKNOWLEDGEMENTS

Unless listed below, the poems included in this volume appear in print for the first time.

Shaun Belcher
'The Ice Horses' previously appeared in *Fatchance 2* in a shorter form
'The Hare-Lip' and 'The Severed Tongue' appeared in *Slowdancer No. 28.*

Tom Bryan
'Diaspora' first appeared in *Wolfwind*, Chapman, Edinburgh, 1996
'George Stephen', first appeared in *North East Passage* (Scottish Cultural Press, Aberdeen, 1996)

Gerry Cambridge
'The Drunken Lyricist' appears in his collection *The Shell House* (Scottish Cultural Press, Aberdeen, 1995)
'The Dark Gift' appears in Gerry Cambridge's little sonnet-book *The Dark Gift.*

Ken Cockburn
'Patchwork Kingdom' previously appeared in *Lines Review*, 133, June 1995

Stewart Conn
'Outsider' and 'Jedibe Camp' previously appeared in *At the Aviary* (Snailpress, Cape Town, 1995)

Christine De Luca
'In the mind's eye' first appeared in an article by Norman R Thomson, 'Landscape, Lives and Literature', in the *Journal of the Scottish Association of Geography Teachers.*
'Hallowe'en hansel' first appeared in *The New Shetlander*

51

Valerie Gillies
'The Rink' previously appeared in *The Ringing Rock* (Scottish Cultural Press, 1995)

John Glenday
'Over Vitebsk' and 'Nimbus' both previously appeared in *Undark* (Peterloo, 1995)

Desmond Graham
'She is learning her hands' previously appeared in *The Marching Bands* (Seren, Bridgend, 1996)
'My Mother Mrs Malaprop' previously appeared in *The Lie of Horizons* (Seren, Bridgend, 1993)

Brian McCabe
'Jenny Long Legs' and 'The Likeness' first appeared in *Lines Review.*

Stuart A Paterson
'Self Portraits' first appeared in *Gairfish* - Overspill
'Old Photographs' first appeared in *Lines Review 132*
'Kingfisher' first appeared in *Carapace* (Republic of South Africa)

Iain Crichton Smith
'The Ghost in the Snow' was published as a broadsheet by Shore Poets, 1995.

Nancy Somerville
'999' has previously appeared in *Past Dancing,* Central Writers' Anthology, 1992; and in *Rich Pickings* (Poetry Now, Peterborough, 1991).

CONTRIBUTORS TO THIS VOLUME

SHAUN BELCHER was born Oxford, England in 1959. Poems published in various magazines including *Oxford Poetry, Gairfish*, etc. At present resident in Edinburgh and still writing songs and drawing and painting, despite the trials of being a temp. in a variety of financial institutions.

TOM BRYAN was born in Canada in 1950. Widely published. Two published poetry collections. Lives in Wester Ross.

GERRY CAMBRIDGE edits *The Dark Horse,* an international poetry magazine with a liking for metre and rhyme.

KEN COCKBURN was born in Kirkcaldy in 1960, and spent time in Germany, France and Wales before settling in Edinburgh. His slim volumes include *Orpheus* (1988) and *Given: Seven Poems, Seven Days* (1995). He is co-editor of *Brilliant Cocophony*, an anthology of writing about Edinburgh.

STEWART CONN's most recent volumes of poems have been *The Luncheon of the Boating Party* and *In the Blood* (both Bloodaxe, Newcastle); and *At the Aviary* (Snailpress, Cape Town). He lives in Edinburgh.

JENNI DAICHES was brought up in the United States and England, and has lived in or near Edinburgh since 1971. She has published literary and social history as Jenni Calder. Her first collection of poetry *Mediterranean* (Scottish Cultural Press) was published in 1995.

CHRISTINE DE LUCA was born and brought up in Waas, Shetland; she now lives in Edinburgh. Writes and performs in Shetlandic and English. First collection 'Voes and Sounds' published by the Shetland Library (1995), nominated for 1996 Shetland Literary Prize. Poems currently being translated into Italian and Swedish.

ANNE C FRATER was born in 1967 on the Isle of Lewis. First poems published in *Gairm* magazine in 1985. Studied Celtic and French at Glasgow University from 1985-1990 and completed a PhD in early Scottish Gaelic women's literature in 1995.

VALERIE GILLIES has published five books of poetry, the most recent being *The Ringing Rock* (Scottish Cultural Press, 1995) which won an SAC Book Award in Spring 1996. Currently she is Writer in Residence at the University of Edinburgh.

JOHN GLENDAY is the author of *The Apple Ghost*, which won an SAC Book Award in 1989, and *Undark*, a PBS Recommendation for 1995. He was appointed the SAC Scottish/Canadian Exchange fellow for 1990/91.

DESMOND GRAHAM lives in Newcastle upon Tyne: two collections from Seren, *The Lie of Horizons* (1993) and *The Marching Bands* (1996); collaborative translation from Polish *Two Darknesses*, Anna Kamienska (Flambard, 1994); recently edited *Poetry of the Second World War: an International Anthology* (Chatto, 1995).

BRIAN MCCABE is a poet, fiction writer, radio dramatist and reviewer. Former Writing Fellow for Ross & Cromarty District Council and has held similar posts for Stirling Libraries and in Strathclyde schools. SAC Scottish/Canadian Exchange Fellow 1988/89.

STUART A PATERSON was born in 1966 in Cornwall, though an Ayrshireman of lang descent. Currently resides in Dumfries where he is Writer in Residence for Dumfries & Galloway. A volume of poems *Saving Graces* is released by Diehard. Is planning a huge expedition of travel, music, poetry in Asia.

TOM POW is the author of three collections of poetry: *Rough Seas*, *The Moth Trap* (Canongate), and *Red Letter Day* (Bloodaxe). He has also written three radio plays, and a travel book on Peru. He lives in Dumfries and teaches at Dumfries Academy.

IAIN CRICHTON SMITH's *Collected Poems* and, most recently, *Ends and Beginnings*, are published by Carcanet. He won the 1994 Forward Prize for the best individual poems (for 'Autumn'), and a 1996 Cholmondeley Award. He lives in Taynuilt.

NANCY SOMERVILLE's work has appeared in various publications. Born in Glasgow in 1953, she began writing poetry and prose ten years ago, and now lives happily in Edinburgh with her two sons, three snakes, and fluctuating numbers of worried mice.